A BIRMINGHAM YANK

A Birmingham Yank

J O H N   G O O D B Y

John Goodby

Arc
PUBLICATIONS
1998

Published by Arc Publications
Nanholme Mill, Shaw Wood Road
Todmorden, Lancs. OL14 6DA

Design by Tony Ward
Printed at the Arc & Throstle Press
Nanholme Mill, Todmorden, Lancs.

ISBN 1 900072 19 X

ACKNOWLEDGEMENTS
Thanks are due to the editors of the following
magazines and anthologies: *Angel Exhaust; Arvon
Anthology 1989; The Cork Anthology; The Honest
Ulsterman; Irish University Review; Krino; London
Magazine; The Observer; Poetry Introduction 8;
Poetry Ireland; Poetry Review; Poetry Wales.*
Thanks also to my brothers Eric and Brian for
providing the story of 'The Raven' and the phrase
'fof story' ('friend of a friend') respectively, and
to Nicola for Keats/Kates and the germ of 'Eighteen
Eighteen'.

The publishers acknowledge financial assistance
from Yorkshire & Humberside Arts Board.

For Katie and George

CONTENTS

JOHN GOODBY was born in Birmingham in 1958, and educated at Hull and Leeds universities. He taught English at Leeds, Cork and Swansea, where he now lives. He is married with two children. His poetry has appeared in many leading poetry journals in the UK and Ireland, as well as in Faber and Faber's *Poetry Introduction 8* (1983).

A Birmingham Yank is his first collection of poems.

I

IN THE TROPICAL HOUSE

The butterflies seem to hatch behind ears,
from hair – the Constable, Paris Peacock,
the Lacewing – as we stray under dripping glass;
you perhaps seeking the White Tree Nymph,
me in attendance on a Bamboo Page.

They might conjure up any possibility,
Magellan's Birdwing, Dark-veined Tiger,
Common Mormon, Postman, Mocker
Swallowtail, as they lazily settle on leaves
or open their books of hours in the shade.

Yet the feather-pronged moths would never feed
in the adult stage. Despite their eye spots
and snake-headed wings, the Giant Atlas,
the Monarch and the Indian Moon Moth
could look to no future except love and famine.

Was the Owl Butterfly a butterfly at all?
You might be a Painted Jezebel on the bridge
above the toy waterfall. I consider it, still
alighting from or on those harder names;
Red Pierrot, Sulphur Emigrant, the Great Duffer.

LORELEY

It seemed that the Rhine slurred her syllables
in a slow dream anschluss with the Liffey,
embracing her like a long-lost sister
to wade into what was the German Ocean
hand in hand. They flowed north-by-north-east
across an England which doesn't exist,
where alder, birch and least willow shadowed
the glacial meltwater.
              Suddenly,
above those cognate streams (the guttural-
together pleasuring of their midstream falls)
she sat on a crag, a glass of black stuff
to hand beside her pack of Sweet Aftons,
whistling 'Only Our Rivers.'
                  My child bride!
Ashore, our tongues would leap one in the other –
yet, from the start, the tone I half-caught
all unenamoured from her song (it poured
like strawberry blond hair from mousey roots);
was fitful; a mixed blitzen that was blind
fool's gold, our disengagement ring's claw-
set antique diamond revealing its flaw
of hesitant anthracite. From her stairs
I saw the Black Church warn, Rathmines Town Hall
plumb the Wicklow peaks with its red tower
more softly than any finger she would wag
and turned away.
             Self-accusations?
I should have danced attendance on her gown,
should never have lost those Fifties court shoes
her *Mutti* handed down. Spilt milk, though; sure –
and when I had been stranded one year shy
of the seven, it had to be time to call
it a day, to steal back down the pebbly shore
where a boat was heeled up above the flood,
the whitewater silence. And shove off,
hearing her whistle again. For what? A wind?
The opening bars of 'The Floating Crowbar'?

STORMING THE WINTER GARDENS

Couldn't-give-a-fuck seventeen in an afghan
playing clock golf, as purple thunderheads
all rhodomontade and patchouli, strolled in
behind applauding waves. The Winter Gardens
reared, tier on red plush tier sussurant
with cash-buckets. I bent, inhaling this line –
taiga, birch sap, codes cracking like birches –
History has made the peasantry its packhorse.

Just the Spring before, Army manoeuvres
at Heathrow had the Queen Mum keeping mum.
Were these our Hot Years – a pre-pre-, even
a pre-revolutionary situation?
No one knew – but crisis was organic:
'Though they may ring the bells now, later
they will wring their hands!' Hands flashed a tic-tac;
'We are the dialectics! Exterminate!'

Above, in their B & B, the Rodrigues
were flying paranoid notices – WE
MUST ASK GUESTS PLEASE DO NOT INTO THE SINK;
WHEN INSPECTORS COME WE NEVER CAN TELL.
They filled the blank frames of *Chilean September*
the cameraman, shot at, shot as he fell –
lumps in throats, we argued more would fall
on film than in our *peaceful transformation.*

Sometime that evening I walked off South Beach
nearly halfway to the Isle of Man. Her
name pursed my lips. The tea-dark Irish Sea
lapped disobligingly below my knees –
it would be harder to drown than I had thought.
Hushed expropriations, dry sobs, nearly-tears –
all night, on the radiator, my flares
clouding in grains of sand and tidemarked salt.

UNDER THE IRON MOUNTAIN

Star Cabs had never heard of that address,
but her sketch on a flayed beer-mat carried me
to a Beeston terrace. Miscegenation!
Our sects could hardly meet except to curse,

so we rehearsed then soothed that schism
with agreed heresies: '"*Late*" capitalism',
I chorused, 'won't be "late" until it's *dead*.'
It was late. We climbed up to her back room.

'When he was fifty my dad learnt Chinese,
or attempted to.' 'A sideways move?'
'My younger brother punched me on the nose
last New Year's Eve.' '– ?' 'This? Apple Mist.'

At dawn, encircled by chill bric-à-brac,
I found my head crooked softly in her arm
and the need for a firmer grip on the facts
growing clearer as she spun fresh yarns.

Of Entrists who sold the 'Workers Bomb'
on the knocker. Of deviant Posadists, who swore
on Marx, Engels and Erich von Daniken.
Red UFOs. And of those who were digging

their own Iron Mountain – who, after war
had wiped the planet, plotted their descent
to history from the cordillera snows.
The tablets of that pure law were unbroken,

but within the week a yucca's pale swords
would bar her kitchen door: turn me back
at futures that still set me wondering
which, if any, were her truest fictions.

HOWLERS

*'We must make it clear to Saddam Hussein
that he has to get out of Northern Ireland.'*
Merlyn Rees, House of Commons, 1991.

Aristotle was the father of philosophy.[1]
                                                              However
this was hardly a comfort to the Seafarer
who suffered badly from metal fatigue, or Hart
Crane, who broke down in the middle of *The Bridge*.
His designs on the short and simple anals of the poor
lead St John Rivers to urge the unwilling Jane Eyre
to take up a missionary position with him

whatever soft incest hangs upon the boughs
as a result. That's Realism – cause and defect –
as clear there as in Chekhov's three best-loved plays
(*The Seagull, The Cherry Orchard* and *The Godfather*),
suggesting that our problems as subjects arose
when Descartes was born in Thomastown, Co. Kilkenny

and Marvell's use of *carpe diem* showed that, for him,
death was inevitable. Shakespeare was tarnished
with the same brush – his funeral baked beans furnished
forth the marriage table – and, reading *Oedipus Rex*,
I am consoled only by the thought that (despite
what one might think) at least the Greeks were not
a morbid people.

[1] Parmenides had a hand in it too.

THE EMPIRE OF ENGLISH

If I write an autobiography it shall be called
Confessions of a Pimp.

Sir Water Raleigh

The lower-classes class it with antimacassars,
    fish-knives, aspidistras; frankly, they're right.
It's unmanly, cashing in on shaming clowns
    in the book-boudoir, or women. Or the darkies
(I taught *them* at the Calcutta Mill in Aligarh
    when my bare name could have shored up the Raj).
It's Greek without tears, jolly-beggar rot
    to liberalise lucre and Philistines
with the *Elegant Extracts* – Keats *did* rot.
    Byron boxed bare-knuckle. Would Bill have glossed
hot flushes for spinsters? "Beget a brat",
    he'd've said, "but don't pule on about your amours."
In the war I offered to get up a hundred
    professors and take on the Boche's best.
(Boche philologists had taken Bill prisoner –
    Coriolanus was packing Junkers in).
We fumed, port-bound. De Selincourt thundered
    that Kaiser Bill was Milton's Father of Lies;
'Q' claimed Hun throats'd choke on iambs.
    Writing should be fighting. Criticism smells.
Let Newbolt mine touchstones for Coketown
    and Ker burn his *Report*. Richards save souls.
I prospect El Dorado – enthusiasms
    for my swill and a gent's fee (guineas down).

NAMESAKES

Although I once drank in Idle Working Men's Club
and know that names are never quite what they seem
it was still hard to swallow Cork Button Co.,
The Iron Throat, a lane called Knapp's Square, a city
which awarded itself the Victoria Cross.

Had that taxi rank been a taxidermist's?
Which church was O'Dwyer's Fire Escape?
One arm of the Lee underwrote Patrick's Street
where the Apostle of Temperance hailed
four hundred and forty-eight bars; the foot-
bridge opened by Lord Mayor Goldberg was said
to have been rechristened The Passover,
the heart-surgery mayor's bridge The Bypass –

yet I still thought then we had learned how Leper's Walk
ran to Lover's Walk, just why the Quadrangle refused
to take four sides. But between the English Market
and the Root Market you slipped past the Butter Market,
before you crossed the Shaky Bridge, broke step.

SHE OF THE NAME

Sweet mortification! The morning suit's
    trousers fitting like a barrel hoop.
    A verse of 'Old Hundredth'
done to death in the pews. Wobbly *I do*s.

In this, the last bedroom we'll ever share,
    I pass back the joint; unstoned
    still, absurd in underwear,
hunkering on the tiled en suite floor

while my heart rings a disconnected tone,
    an *epithalamium,*
    epithalamium. I'm
the sick, sick Brother of the Groom,

my silk-purple consort She of the Name,
    though in name now only:
    'Bovine' and 'Bevin'
it has been; once, amazingly, 'Bahrein'.

Who'd believe that for my twenty-eighth
    she purloined Untermeyer's
    Life of Heinrich Heine?
That she'd thaw her feet of ice at my groin

through winter nights in our back-to-back?
    Though we never lay back to back
    our ends have been shaped
by destiny, rough-hew it how she would

with those unkeepable parting vows–
    to be as if 'sister', 'brother' –
    made in bright May weather
before the last, family-only photos.

A BESTIARY

i The Mole

So long sapping, I became my elements –
dirt, roots, galleries walled with smoke.

They matched those of mine enemies,
but what dawned when the roof-tree broke

was the wrong light, had been betrayed
and split; was not the light inside.

As I lay buried, some underhill haled
me out with tongs and had me crucified.

Now, *I* won't cry if we start from scratch –
I grant all the above as a first premise –

as long as *you* promise you'll leave
The Wind in the Willows out of this.

ii The Wren

Christ's stool pigeon, the wren-boys' *droleen*
in sweaty Gethsemane; it blurts
its silver for a centurion's ear
minutes before the snatch squad goes in.

iii The Snail
after Giusti

They say you have rather a lot
to be modest about,
but telescopes, spiral stairs
and dented shields are your spin-offs.

And you count your blessings,
Diogenes of your order:
you need venture no further
than your threshold's false foot

17

to savour the air; you avoid
all panics and pandemics.
So much for Beijing or Paris!
You chew a homelier cud.

There are those who snort
and bluster, who can't be kind.
Not you; you toe the crooked line
of your iridescent snot,

since nature has been lavish
in her gifts (headsmen,
take note – shellityhorn
decapitated will regraft).

View him, then, through rose-
tinted, not grotesque, spectacles;
render unto Caesar,
play follow my leader;

and you'll soon be caught out
whistling his numbers,
'Pink Flag' or 'Cwm Rhondda',
hearing his "We're *alright*!"

IV THE RAVEN

She was disembowelling a bin-bag;
I was casting a butcher's at the local rag

just days before they crossed the border
in the Shell/Texaco/Gulf War.

I watched her flap, stiffly, to my shoulder.
Her talons gripped to the bone

as she leant to impart this fof story
about a fleet of artics shuttling

freezer containers around the clock
at that almost-midnight hour

to a warehouse on a disused dock
somewhere upriver of Canary Wharf.

v THE HARE

Dew-beater, stag of the cabbages, shagger,
seven-and-seventy-named furze-cat –
kiss her kibe for luck as she doubles back
across stubble-fires, swerves straight
through a hedge-hole. To rise, Hare of the Moon.
Though they say "Wat" is enough
to keep men ashore, even if her scut
once plugged the stoven belly of the Ark,
do we take her lip, glimpsing the arch
over water of the beginning glyph?
Keep mum about grandma on her hearth
that day? The pool of blood in her lap?

vi THE SEAL-POINT SIAMESE

After that, no *Daily Worker*
sales in New Street,
no fraternal greetings,
an old man's tea socialized
at weekly Branch meetings.

My Tankie uncle thumps his hand:
"Stick to the line. On
your own you're *nothing*."
"So what happened to the thaw?"
Someone opens the door

on the struggle by other
means. And ten years on
I hear my younger brother call
from the porch not 'Si' or 'Am'
but 'Viet? Viet Cong?'

OF THE BOOK

Her little granny boots that broke his heart to bits –
they kick off this film, *The Summer of the Esses* –
Sally, Shirley 'Shome Mishtake', 'Crêpes' Suzette –

and click-clack past six drained pints of *mea culpa*
exiting a bar. Brick Lane. Dust. Gnawed B-B-Q ribs
in gutters. The day wavering in the August heat

but not her resolve, tested near the Museum of Labour,
or Childhood, as they part (he descends Bethnal tube –
briefly, we should think: *third rail*.) And cut to a phone

in a baked, empty room that rings and dies for her.
Some distance off, still wearing his ring, she
touches it and smiles aloud. All those *years*! A bench

outside The Swan With Two Nicks (or Necks) next;
another girl is recalling how, not so long back,
he wolf-whistled Bach, watching *The Apartment*

with her, more The Creeping Hand than *mensch*.
But now she pities his Nick Carraway hair. Now
his rendition of 'White Man At The Hammersmith Palais'

falters in the northern air. Dodging traffic
and a shower near her cottage (the First Night scene cut
with good reason), his new docs blistering him already,

he limps for anywhere open. A bookshop doorbell
I Ching-ching-chings. The final shot, watch him pick out
that old cream and orange Penguin, *The Horse's Mouth.*

BOSOLA IN LOVE
for Steve Gale

True, madonna, I am the only court-gall –
as lecherous, covetous, proud as any man –
though a scholar at Padua once, a fantastical
seeker of what colour was Achilles' beard,
the number of knots in Hercules' club,
whether Hector had toothache; one who studied
the symmetry of Caesar's nose, half blear-eyed,
and measured it against a shoeing horn.

Now, like a foul porpoise before the storm,
I lift my snout: but your familiars
(mere roaring boys who eat meat seldom)
have digg'd up the mandrake that I hear shriek
and the wells at Lucca must purchase your cures
for strong-thighed bargemen, or the pistoles
plunged by your Switzer in his great codpiece.
Your stirrup is riveted through their noses.

Quit your palace of sycophants. It is rumoured
you are a night-walker, a poisoned Spanish fig.
(Gentlemen o'the wood-yard, she's exposed!)
Didst thou never study the mathematics?
How does your time pass? (O loose i'th'hilts,
cannibal, see what the devil can do!)
Cover yourself in cloth-of-gold, in silks,
a Jew's spittle still makes the richest tissue.

Excellent hyena! Spurn me, I'll crawl after,
a sheep-biter, though ears stopped with black wool
are deaf to my howling. I haunt churchyards
like a lycanthropy. Even so, I would
flay this face like a nutmeg-grater
or abortive hedgehog to charm eyes that dazzle,
to witness your common fountains shed
their few pure silver-drops in general.

EX LIBRIS

In your *Art of Henry Moore*, my inscription gloats
'From one reclining nude to another' –
worse, that, than the *Atlas of Revolutions*
with your 'Hoping our turn comes next year',
or the other book I still keep from you, *The Past*.
Do you keep the *History of the Commune*
by 'Lissa', the fiancé Tussy Englished
and dropped; unread, kept because it is unread?
Let it part at that map of *arrondissements*,
Haussmanned, scarlet-inked, its Banque de France
virginal before the blood, toil, sweat, and Thiers'
Sacré Coeur. Even open – see? – a closed book,
though once (years ago now) you'll swear you heard
faint groans oozing from its freshly-turned earth.

IN THE MUSEO CESARE BATTISTI
for Síle Ó Hora

I'd sweated up the Doss, the local hill,
whose sylvan path gyres
to a tonsured crown
and gawped over the town
from its colonnaded, unroofed marble sweep –
then suddenly skedaddled
for the dimness
of a museum-crypt
under white birdshot, pelting cisalpine hail.

That day you'd 'denounced' me in the castello
to the third – or was it the fourth? –
arm of an octopus law.
You'd frowned in consternation
as pigeons clattered, blurring *al fresco* frescos.
The Duomo still wore
dark pasts on its sleeve –
a boy-martyr's carved-up tears,
the quangos of the Counter-Reformation.

In the square Neptune goaded his fountain,
self-saddled, a sea-centaur
with a gilt toasting-fork:
"So far, the tideline
of the gift of Two Fish is stuck at Verona;
but this town's cards are marked – "
you'd stopped. Dead-dog-
and-tree-trailing, Adige
roared, a sullen joyrider from the mountains.

Mountains? Migraine heights, cloud-bandaged peaks
rather, where the Dolomites'
faint pink granites
should have flushed and glowed
each evening; for one entire March week
they shook their rain-shadow.
Dolor! Fat, regular
blood-warm drops blackened
the Street of the Orphans each day at four.

All week, too, in the dark, time-switched stairwell
it seemed as if I heard
a bird – soft yellow,
flame-like, an imaginary bird –
turn and turn in its rusted, protesting
wheel of song (did
it gibber all day long?)
Outside, the foothills were untwisting
in rain, their sheet-rope streams fraying into mist.

Sat in your blind kitchen, savouring frottage
of garlic on the toast, charred
and bristled with anchovies
pink-grey as the Art Deco
station, or sweet, rabbit-punching coffee
and endless Stuyvesaants,
it all looked black –
coffee, tobacco, the megrims –
in what had once been Austrian Italy

to a spry self-pitier, glum bat-self, swung
like a bell, his gaped *O*s
thirsting for a sign.
O mother-of-pearl tongue
lisping back, filmed with blue fire, grappa-blue!
Its peasant skin was grape-skins.
Its pips were the residue
left by the cardinals
to be distilled, bitter and tridentine,

to the dumb, gravid fluid tongues might weep.
I sipped a wordless vertigo
for highs and lows,
for love, that *Absolutism*
tempered by slovenliness (suave Adler
on the walrus monarchy –
a Wildean rejoinder,
a sweet, glittering plum
in the porridge of nation and socialism).

When he voted war, Adler soaped the noose
for his Trento deputy –
Cesare's mutiny (later
to be hijacked by il Duce)
was his caesura: Vienna's trap dropped
to this whited memorial,
a lost son served up
among crumbling refuse,
the bat-shit of the Second International –

too Austro for Italy then, too Latin
for me; hung in shrouds
as epochs crashed gears
(dumpling-fascists still bombing the line
to Bozen, though routes to their 'black' south run clear),
I steamed in religious light,
shivering, waiting to go
back up to the white clouds
letting rip and that sprawling, fish-eyed view.

II

TINTERN ABBEY

'But for splendour and beauty of scenery, what I have yet seen of Ireland
is not to be compared to Scotland, the North of England, or Wales.'
Wordsworth, 1829

Passed under Vinegar Hill two nights before,
the Tintern Abbey he might have sought out
would be hunched at Bannow Bay, Co. Wexford.
Whether or not it impressed is a moot point

after the *over-celebrated Scalp, too-famous
Powerscourt, the meeting of the two Avons
which was charming, but by no means equal
to the Fascally, Garry or Tummel* (he'd call

a thing that ran to thirteen books a 'prelude').
O, tautologous, the *disappointing scenery*!
Gulphs of solipsism ! Hadn't he once viewed
it in terror? Wept, wrestled walls and trees

before she supplemented them? *Her* resolution
troped independence in stars, stones, violets;
now rebel nature seeded her profusion –
Conspiracies against landlords and magistrates,

the buddleia smoking purplish from a garret,
a bridge with fallen arches. Dorothy will read,
clacking the nasty plates of her Waterloo teeth,
at Rydal Mount, and in starched discomfiture

stray back to the pig blood-panelled parlour
in what was recently The Dove and Olive.
Pitt has just declared war on Thermidor
and, after five days solid of her porridge,

recalling Johnson's entry under 'Oats',
Scott has unbolted the guestroom window
and will cross four meadows to the Swan Inn
where they lay on a lairdly roast beef and claret.

Snow wipes the children's foreheads where they sleep.
The octogenarian fire soughs white ash.
Glassily, she quizzes that odd sock fished up
from the depths of her copper in the last Great Wash.

BLOW-IN

One night, in pitch-dark horizontal rain,
I'll drive that last mile by touch
and touch alone. The jouncing track
will end at what was a whistle-stop
on a superannuated branch line.

You'll talk of having been up since dawn
to nail down slates, massacre
monkey puzzles in the nettled acre;
of how, despite blue thumbs,
you've been overrun by runner beans.

Platform One is grass. The waiting room
is as blank, now, as that daily round
swapped for a life of spiders; here
the diaspora of cadres fades
like smirr into your local mountain.

One wall is still ribbed with big lives;
another warps around an Aga.
Owl-light frames a door left ajar
on the last train from Macroom,
the next last industrial revolution.

THE DEATH OF LITTLE NELL

Lord Jeffrey wept 'like a girl'. Macready's diary
was tear-slubbered. The Liberator, overcome,
hefted his copy of *The Old Curiosity Shop*
through an open window on the Derrynane down train.
Heartstring-plucker himself, he should have been
as hard as that steel-hasped tome; it glanced my temple,
made me see stars and sent me sprawling, winded
across the marble slab of Chapter Seventy One...

A sloe-mole on her right cheek. Blond, elflocked fringe.
Blue-veined milk-and-water skin. Hedgerow lips
starved thin on stewed nettles, filched raw yolks, haws.
High Tartar cheekbones whetted by weeks on the run
from a man with a wax hand or a wooden leg.
"I sold posies for ha'pence", she said, "held horses.
Begged. As if I were Judy I bore up my Punch
and we both toed the line of some improbable plot.

"On the Grand Union the bargees brawled and diced
at Dutch Hazards and Old British. They shared their bread,
but only if I would toast Saint Monday in max.
After five I was 'Eskimo O'Nell'; one offered
to jump over brush and steel and live with me tally.
They all kipped dead drunk, piked over tow-ropes, snoring
to waken Hades. But if they knew Cradely and Clonmel
my mossed Shropshire village hardly rang a bell."

She had stuck to their north-by-north-west. More canals
than Venice at last debouched in Gas Street Basin.
She left water for earth, for pillars of smoke and fire.
"Home was no refuge. Peel's brimstone reduced us
to kindling for the Limbo Dancers' children's crusades.
From the Liberties to São Paulo their angel
factories and scabbed flues might stretch to the moon,
but never to societies to protect the born child."

She was fading as I blinked up into the blue
ache of a sky that never rains but it pours.
Water from a top hat sloshed my face. Whistles
scolded, and blood and brandy scalded my slack mouth.
A goatee'd samaritan loomed like the dickens,
hissed "Ellen!" and tuned on his cleft heel. Staunched,
· I continued for Clontarf. Then, fifty miles out,
riders began bringing the news we could not credit.

Moral force had scotched the monster. Now success
in crying down Chartists would call down potato blight,
men of tin disperse Kennington and the petition
signed 'Mister Punch', the Iron Duke's clubbable peelers
pluck Bronterre to defeat from the jaws of victory.
Her last words had been whispered: "The Hampton Road
is dinned with forges; but already I hear crowds
jostling on New York quays for news of my death."

ONE OF THE PTOLEMYS

Twelve pianos were flinging 'La Violette'
upstairs and down. Our guide, Sister Two-Eight,
smiled her saint's smile. Do Ursulines flagellate?
Use hairshirts? Oubliettes? I'd read Diderot,
I shivered in the sun in their kitchen-garden.
(And how do they move? On *castors*? Be Magdalens,
I say, before you kneel at that wicket – sheeted
furniture of heaven, Suttee-hearts immolated!)

Queasy, I left for God's air, the river strolling
by freely, at a man's pace. The dollies
were keening Higos in the typhus holds
of transports; shawlies and stumpy doodeens
idled on Patrick's Bridge. In their cabins
they'd lie in bed all day 'for the hunger'.
(*I'd* go without on Friday, with its four fish –
fish fried, fish raw, fish stinking and ling!)

The Coal Quay shows they'd rather die than pray
or stuff County stirabout – scarecrow-gear,
stalkoes crying hoops, bottles, nails. Ignore
scenery or art; the Sublime of Want
sells Croker's *Tours* and Lover's *Character*.
They starve a stone's-throw from the scuffed array
of the Mardyke; all gloom, but for a red butcher
calling us back to buy some 'honest meat'.

The 'tyrant sister kingdom', then? Yet laws
didn't spoil their Art School for want of a brush,
or cobweb the libraries of a book-crazed town,
or leave temples unporticoed. It's as much
the braggadocio starts, indolent trailings off

*   *   *   *   *   *   *   *

Palmyra's sadness, Thebes-gated thistle-fields,
walls fissile with hart's-tongue and maidenhair.

I laughed and cried – street arabs' chatter ranged
to *one of the Ptolemys* – but saw-millers
were milling at the vitriol-flingers trial
as we galloped out; a place without change
for a five pound note, like our fire, sulking
until Peggy brought up coals – in a CHINA PLATE!
(its coal-dusted head the Queen's, or my wife's,
still bonneted, bobbing in the packet's wake).

HARRIET SMITHSON'S JULIET

I

We were both slaves to the Ape of Genius,
an irlandaise and her fool. Who succumbed
to whom? By Act III I was breathing hard;
an iron hand had squeezed my heart (O for a heart
of iron!) to the pulp of a poperin pear
before I blundered out through Le Tourneur's
alexandrine fog. Satan had sent Shakespeare,
but for once no one asked for a refund.

I would play Hamlet myself, true: sulk over
The Loves of the Angels; be translated
to dewfalls, citrus dusks... I was a lover
then, and stank, and wore clogs carved from firewood,
and dreamt of conducting cannonades,
of hurling myself on kettledrums. Episodes
in the life of an artist? Try more mustard,
leeks, bread, oil, salt, vinegar, cheese and lard.

II

That gentleman with the eyes that bode no good
was a sham ballox burning at my stage-door.
When Romeo kissed me, his brouhaha would
upstage the Monument Scene with a scene in the stalls.
When I told him flowers were homage enough
he whinnied, white-eyed, and gnawed at his buttonhole.
When the manager saw that he flapped our contracts
at us, declaiming them like the Riot Act.

III

About this time I lost the power to sleep
(it is a power, as you will discover when
you lose it yourselves). Alright, so I did sleep
occasionally. But only three times. Four then.
One night near Ville-Juif on sheaves and stubble;
once, in daylight, in a field outside Sceaux;
once, in the snow, beside the frozen Seine
near Neuilly. And last, at a zinc-topped table

36

in the Café du Cardinal, Boulevard
des Italiens, where for five hours the waiters
dared not approach me for fear I was dead.
One power was still left me – to suffer –
and I marched to the scaffold for her murder.
A sour wineglass shivered in a homeless key;
the dawn-breeze woke. Awnings drummed. A viola
descending the Alps sang Ireland in Italy.

ARIOSTO
after Mandelstam

It's cold now in Europe. In Italy it's dark.
Power, with a barber's hairy paws,
strokes the nape of the neck. So, throw open
a window on the lulled Adriatic, on bees

stumbling between musk-roses, the campagna
fidgety with crickets. The sun gongs noon.
Hippogriff prints steam, crescent, in the turf.
Lift the golden dumb-bell of the hourglass.

In the language of cicadas, a woozy blend
of Pushkinian sadness and *sprezzatura*,
he buttonholes us, incorrigible,
and fibs heroically about Orlando,

kind old Ariosto. A pure reynard, fern-whorl,
sail-stitcher, agave – from the moon
he reported the yellowhammer's song
and on dry land became an instructor to fish.

Soulless, lizard city! Lumpen Ferrara,
you spawned such sons from a judge and a witch;
bitted, harnessed them on a choker rein.
Like red-maned suns they lit the wilderness.

Look, the lamb is white against the hill-fold.
A monk jogs by on his ass. The Duke's Switzers,
daft with wine and garlic, itch their buboes.
A sausage stall flaps in the shade. A child dozes.

He grins from a balcony, playing the great man.
He addresses oceans, virgins. He clews
us through the maze of chivalric scandal,
dizzy with marvels as we are at our loss.

THE KING OF FLOWERS

He had heard the comet sputter 'Poltava'
and die; ever since, the state's banked fires
hissed science, vivisectionists and priests.
Livonia was old hat now. Hats fought Caps

in the gloom, canons coughed up purer elements –
cobalt, nickel, manganese. Taking orders
in beasts, in the lilies of the field
('Tobacco is five husbands with one wife'),

he would sleepwalk like Swedenborg's dead
in a world that still limped on flower feet;
his apostles scattered like thistledown
as he spied from the library on his hands,

and when river-mists crawled the orangery,
the King of Flowers begged a new retreat
from his ornamental king. His king said *No*,
and sent a patent of nobility.

He wept then, inconsolable as an onion.
Fate took her measure, but was all God's work
for mankind's use? His farthest bodies?
Again he gulped urine, warm from the herds,

stomaching. Eyes cataracted like the skies.
Twenty-four classes shinned up smoke-ladders
to his two-faced name as it dribbled bronze
from thickets scrimshandered on a Lapp *bodhrán*.

LORDS OF THE NAVIGATION

'And if there had been more of the world,
they would have reached it.' – Camões

I

There was no such god as Jupiter, but I saw
his wind raise hackles on the Sea of Straw
where caravels strained for the Great Fish River.

The Romanus Pontifex chartered it
after waylaid Crusaders stopped off for loot –
so forget the Twelve of England, forget 'proof'

João was descended from Tubal – it was
Gaunt's daughter who blooded the House of Aviz;
Ceuta was gutted with English expertise,

but revealed that our own homes were pigsties.
With that we tracked the Negus, keelhauled the Cape
to style ourselves Lords of the Navigation.

II

Da Gama fell on Calicut. Arabs jeered
"What devil's shit brings you here?" "Spices
and Christians. Here, a gift for your Samorin –

this crew of his, diced, for his next pullao."
We dipped ledgers in the blood of the Lamb;
our doubting hands foraged India's side

and Saint Thomas's Syriacs baptised
a scratch empire of *entrêpots,* traders' scurf
from Ormuz to Malacca. As for Castille,

we say, *When a man's field is narrow his cow*
will mank his neighbour's pasture. They can follow,
as long as they don't call us Galicians.

III

Once I was Trustee for the Dead and Absent
in Macau, amanuensis for tales
of birds that gobble iron, anthropophagi,

tribes that inhale only the scent of flowers –
they were nautch-girls' gossip, cannabis mists.
After Sebastião know this, and this alone:

that the first, and first last, will be first again;
that the boy with genitals like a radish
and what vanished like hail off a wadi

at El-Kebir will grab the earth by its balls;
that my salt epic packs its flesh, whatever sways
the Hidden One's Avalon or Hy Brasil.

THE CHIEF ENGINEER

Before Barbarossa, the ten-month winters
thawed; but by then my first wife's hair was ash.
OGPU dropped 'parasite', and Star City
fell in a yellow-starred potato patch.

But first, I busked fugues on Stalin's Würlitzers
from Kursk to Peenemünde. "Don't shoot, Ivan!"
they wept at Stand X, "*scientists*! Not *Nazis*!"
I crated them east with *Vergeltungswaffen*.

Years. Then October bit Newton's apple
and wedged in Yankee throats, JANFUs butter-
fingered von Braun's 'grapefruit', all j-jitters,
as Sputnik backcombed Berenice's hair.

And last, ice-smouldering, gantries fell back
from my Little Eagle. R-7 shook.
Engines that hissed like samovars flared
brewing up a sunrise over Baikonur:

Cedar – this is Dawn One! Like Caesar's Gauls
my children thought the sky might break their heads.
They broke my heart. Hems rose to them, vodka,
fanfares. Under their heels I was steppe-mud.

In Spring I came to heel under Khruschev's –
that *muzhik* Rumpelstiltskin! – and dispersed
in his 'triumph of our peace-loving peoples';
a Pheibos or Deimos press-ganged by Mars.

Statues only attract pigeons – Lenin.
Who was right, but willed us hunger and ice.
When I was cyphered God blew raspberries
through the eternal silences of space.

Now they say MAD was my one aim. I say
the champagne of stars will toast real heavens –
let a white dwarf then weigh my heavy names
in lights: Sergei Pavelich Korolyev.

IN ST AMBROSE'S
after Giusti

Excellence, though you think me anti-Austrian
when my targets are fools and turnip-heads to refer
to the slurry of Danubian jakes, dilate
on the unnatural fondness of Magyars for their mares,
listen; idling in town one parched forenoon
last week (minding other people's business
for you) I happened to slip into Saint Ambrose's,
a crumbling old chapel just off the piazza.

Don't ask why. I was gooseberry for the day
to a son of that Santo the novelist who wrote
I Promessi Sposi, a work your Excellency
looks as if he's never read. Never *heard* of?
Christ and his angels... No, it's a bagatelle.
Your Excellency's mind – God grant His servants
ineffable peace and a sense of proportion –
is engrossed by more than mere literature.

It was like a barracks inside. Every rank
from general down to drummer-boy was there, each one
of them an Austro – Bohemian or Croat
espaliers stuck here in God's own vineyard –
all at attention, ramrods up arses, tow-
moustached faces stiff as spindles, eyes *Front*!
as if God Almighty were court-marshalling them.
I kept the wall; but I wasn't wary enough

to keep *this* buttoned. One good gulp and the dry
heaves hit me (your post spares you such indignities),
though mercifully I was unbreakfasted. *Why*?
Because of the sudden stench of horseblankets,
greased puttees, cabbage soup, the biscuity sweetness of
                            sweat,
because – beg pardon Excellence – in that house of God,
even as the host blanched at its elevation
the candles seemed to drool and stink of suet.

But as the monstrance dropped there was a strange
apologetic wheeze from under the altar;
an oompah band! Cornets. Fifes. A paunchy tuba.
A brass and silver burnishing of note after note
from ploughshares beaten out of swords of song, the voice
of a people suppliant in their tribulation –
you know, that Verdi chorus the Lombards chant
to heaven, proud, unslaked, sorrowful, that "O Lord,

from the Houses of our Birth" (the one scored
on our hearts in our Italian Babylon...)
It transported me. I lost the thread of myself
in the blind gripe and backwash of the thing:
as if it had made those untouchable others
people of our people, flesh of our flesh, I swayed
and blundered deeper into the crowd. Unnerving
isn't the word for it – granted the piece is fine,

is ours, was well-performed – for the way great art
occasionally transcends honest-to-goodness
bigotry. Even as the dying fall shivered
the nave my prejudice returned, sure as quails
in spring from the sea. And *then* from those mouths –
mouths like the blond mouths of dormice – one last
chorale began to slowly creak aloft
through the red-eyed smokes of myrrh and sandalwood,

a bat-winged, crepuscular lament, beseeching;
loam-ecstatic, fir-resinous, reproachful
as those songs that cost you your childhood, the cud
the heart chews when tears are its daily bread,
as riddled with sadness for a sister, a mother,
as a cheese is with mites. Divine harmony,
how could you work against such a stubborn grain!
Rapt, giddy, drunken, dizzying, it trembled

to a close; and the after-râle made thought tender,
fortified its iron over an anvil's beak.
And I knew: they've been uprooted by a Hapsburg
so shit-scared of his wops and woodentops cutting loose
that he starves them, press-gangs them, whips them here
like slaves to keep us as slaves – herds them down
from Croatia and Bohemia, the way flocks
are herded south in winter to the Maremma.

What's their life after all? Rations. Drill. Flogging.
Leper garrisons where their RSMs terrify
more than we ever could. The gagged mechanics
of imperial plunder (and not one blackened
scudo greases their palms), they barely know
it happens. We trade them hate for hate; we whet the blade
of divide and rule, fret out the paranoid jig-
saw that carves out our leaguing against the king.

So call me bleeding heart; I pitied them. Forlorn,
loathed – when who knows but that deep down they're not
thinking "Stuff the Emperor" too? And I swear
if I hadn't suddenly barged out at this point
I'd've turned and bear-hugged a corporal stood
right where you are now, with his hazel swagger-
stick jammed under his armhole, his dusty boot-heels
kissing. Bound fast to the stake of himself.

FOR THE COMMISSION OF THE FIVE

Saved from brother fire, six feet of mother earth,
I passed down the Rat Line in disguise to Rome.
Sister water I have crossed to a refuge
half-water; I am 'Professor Anic', lodged
in a bolt-hole from Reds for the Holy See.
I see only Minorites. I have no talk,
though Brother Luji visits me from Galway –
sad in a neutral state, in a strange country
which will not shoot striking milkmen or invade
its lost Northern province, every breakfast
he spoons down jar after jar of damson jam
and, through jam-whiskers, curses Broz. I worry
for him, for you; for us all. Any day now,
he says, the West will declare World War Three.

At the end of each day, by the Grand Canal
under the purple hills, wrung-out Atlantic skies,
to the sparking of a Rathgar trolleybus
evening is a turquoise lift, a turf-smoke sigh –
a damp copy of the bright squares of Kaptol,
of the fluent Sava, the Una and Strug
chattering in our Croat, our Gothic tongue
debauched by Muslims, by Orthodox (our words
never started wars over the price of pork).
The Irish let their language slip through their hands;
they speak shameless English, in which 'soil' and 'dirt',
the terms for 'earth', can also mean 'pollution'
(unlike the true ground of our speech, which I scoured
of Gypsy, Jew and Slav in my lexicon) –

yet they know, like us, great art is national.
In the War, I would tell them, I banned *Hamlet*
but not the pure Irish *Riders to the Sea*.
Neue Europa would have twinned our two states –
we share love of the land, Church, past oppression.

O'Brien, the Papal Count, is exalting us
as the Saviours of Christendom from the Turk
(just as in darkness, Ireland once saved the faith).
But I leave soon. I can balance books. The friars
have made me an accountant in America.
Pay my tributes to Cardinal Ruffini
but remember; Poverty is my new bride,
and the thirty-four chests of teeth and watches
under the deaf-and-dumb confessional are yours.

THE KALIF OF CONAMARA

The Tree of Life, they said, puts down twin roots
through Ibn al-Bawaab and the Book of Kells;
beneath Galway boughs their last hookahs fumed
as they praised the Berber ululations of *sean-nós*.

Lateen-rigged *púcáns*, we were told, would bear us clear
round Jab al-Tariq, sea-courses set
trine by their stars – Rigel, Aldebaran, Altair –
to make a landfall beyond Byzantium.

Like ours, their Paradise is only for men.
Curd-fleshed houris, their virginities renewed
immaculately forever, attend each silk divan
beside spring-waters fluent as Mozarabic weave.

We are sick of turf smoke under thatch, weather-
agues, vinegar wine and black-faced priests;
the shamrukh is the sceptre of empire;
Saint Patrick was our first imperialist.

We shall return to the Land of the Fathers.
Our mackerel will shoal into flying fish.
The Tallaght Martyrology's seven monks
will be buttered with Copt nard and frankincense.

Our women may take the veil. We have embarked
cured beef, oatmeal, water-skins, pigs and poets
to explicate immrama, under a guard
of Sligo Dragonskins. The people have danced

a battering for hours through to this last dawn.
I trace the *Bism'illah* on my cruciform brooch,
hearing our dolphin-escort cry out from the Shannon
'Issa' or 'Iosa', it hardly matters which.

MONTSÉGUR

I PERFECT ONES

Whose pretext, then, for this Crusade? The Pope's?
His Legate's blood had already soaked
Béziers, necklaced in its purple tripes.

Justice mocked 'oc' with de Montfort, *for*
if one may seek Christ Jesus by slaying women
and slitting children's windpipes

he must needs find a crown in heaven. "Your Grace,
how will we know heretics from believers?"
A growl; then, "Kill them *all.* God will know his own."

II SPIRITUALS

Approaching from the north-west, from Foix,
the skinners enfiladed limestone
gorges and splashed across the Aude

to invest Montségur. But weeks passed. Months. When
all else had failed, Franciscans were sent
to dispute. But these stood upwind of them:

"So devout, even the Holy Father thinks
you stink like pigsties. When your work is done,
you will also bend or be burnt. Now, 'rejoice'."

III TROUBADOURS

At last, in Spring, *perfecti* dragged like bees
from their cells. Two hundred and seventy five
for the stake (seventeen made the night before,

knowing this: *Yes. I am one of them. Burn me.*).
The *credentes* limped home. Free to bugger,
so rumour said, their pigs; to find new grief

in daughters who had begun to wander.
Their songs impure, ravished. Who would breathe
this lavender air and not some other.

49

WITH THE BLUE DEVILS

'I would have told all my Irish friends
their freedom was coming.'
                              – Helmut Clissman

The *Examiner* cheered O'Duffy from Cork;
Hogan penned *Will Ireland Go Communist?*
St John Gogarty spat at 'yids' as he walked
down Sackville Street – last of the great wits,
he dived in the Liffey once, taking a piss.
Joyce skewered him, but his namesake haw-hawed
after Yeats read in a neon BOVRIL sign
death agonies of the Gaelic Weimar
(for the sake of blood Yeats farted blue devils,
though it's said he never said 'gaberdine swine.')

The Stockholm of the West gasped out its news –
Hitler's 'thirst for international justice'.
Mad England offered to twist Craig's arm.
Éire, cool, refused. England would lose. Now spies
flit like a *spéirr-bheann*'s Stuart from coast
to coast, the Dáil hears: "The Blitz is a judgement
on English materialism!" Up to speak,
Flanagan tables an emergency motion
on the Jews "who once crucified our Saviour
and crucify us now every day in the week".

In the Red Bank bar's cellar they knuckled down
to oysters, swastikas, chewing the fat:
"Let the Nazis invade the North – who'd know
different? These SS are just glimmer men
in uniforms…" On Westmoreland Row
the Reich Embassy shuffled flower pots
and from Balina strand a Sikh Abwehr oppo,
like some Axis Mannanán, would stumble
into a bar and order (this is true)
"A pint of whiskey!", his *blas* impeccable.

'Skulking'? Perhaps, though Francis in Berlin
wasn't Frank in Dresden the night they smashed
the bone china. Russell, that ruined Casement,
opened to Ribbentrop; but Chamberlain
signed him a blank cheque, and his replacement
(last heard of dyeing the Dardanelles red)
had prayed for "an English Führer" in defeat
"to return us to our rightful place among
the nations", and kept Home Guards square-bashing
with loaded broom stales in England's Garden.

EIGHTEEN EIGHTEEN

'What a thing would be a history of her life and sensations' – Keats

Her breath of rampions, quids and old middens
shrivelled him like a sybil's breath as she bent lower
from her pole-slung kennel borne by two handmaidens
in their worse than nakedness of the Irish poor.

"Kates? Keats? Yeats? Yates? It must be you I seek,
poet, although your gyre has not yet unwound":
suddenly she pissed fit to lay the summer dust
six miles from Bangor to Donaghadee.

"I am Ireland", she crooned, "great is my bladder.
Know that the second Jew is come this year;
his marks appear plain in the pikes of Down
and Antrim, the lost, third strike of the weavers,

and in the Belfast shuttle's disgusting noise
that will weft and warp the world." She was squab,
half-starved from scarcity of biscuit, an ape
from Madagascar shipping for the Cape

who eyed the Scotch mist over Ailsa Craig
for some clearer sign. "Your voice is Yola,
and, although you wear the butcher's apron,
you stain it in the service of Apollo.

Weep subversively. There will be no more truth
until Dunluce Castle goes down on its knees
to the tides and the Sea's Swallow, until
we bury each twisted weasel's mislaid tooth;

take your text from our totem poles that spell
GOD IS LOVE by THE WICKED SHALL BE TURNED
Into HELL, take it all with a pickle o'salt:
until then I remain the Duchess of Dunghill."

He bowed. She spat tobacco juice; whistled, lurched off
in her sedan. His friend turned to him then
and saw his silent howl widening as if
standing for *Christ's Entry Into Jerusalem.*

A BIRMINGHAM YANK

"August 1914; forget the rest –
for the first time *the chassis moves past
the workman*. Soon, they re-invent
the wheel as one hundred separate tasks,

split Spic from Swede, Kraut from Kike.
Basic wage $5 a day,
three shifts, no breaks. It's Taylor,
PPS and the Pinkertons. Drink?"

Right then we saw flash an Iron Cross
with Oak Leaves, First Class,
from Herr Hitler (first name 'Heil')
and knew he could buy and sell

the pub, the station, the whole village
of Ballinascarthy. We drank all day
to that Birmingham Yank; any
colour he liked as long as it was black.

III

A BIRMINGHAM YANK

THE MISSING LINK

Drenchings, thunderbox death-grunts and sulphur
enough to blacken the apostle spoons – what
did he *do* in there half the morning? I lurked
on the landing, *ur*-Hamlet; longhaired, but girl-
smooth still. My eyes looked daggers at his back
as he burst forth with "'I could a fart unfold
whose lightest breath/Would harrow up thy soul!'"
I entered his stinking steam, his absences.

Four nights, three, then two a week he'd linger
at home no longer home. Lean, spartan, he ate
strange flesh – flummery slashed with black treacle
(*out of the strong came forth sweetness*); phallic-
clitoral gherkins; raw eggs, exquisitely blown.
He scoured his teeth with salt on a forefinger.
Once, he'd just lived on Guinness for a fortnight,
but emptied their only barrel, and lost a stone.

Near the end, when my career as a burglar
ended on scaffolding, he pulled strings – some
Old Bill mates, a brief, a Clouseau mac, a saw –
'Drink is a good servant but a bad mashter' –
and failed. His careers advice was disastrous,
to be a police pathologist. Come autumn
I was going to Cambridge Heath Road, not
Cambridge; then, making black smoke, up North.

Before I could leave he left with his books
(bound in wallpaper, they crossed the city
more in sorrow than in anger, more in self-pity
than either). To me, he had commended
'your mother' in a croak – *Who's died,* I think
I thought, *you?* – but then spent a weekend
at his new place, passed off as the builder's boy,
to seal a lyric, quisling summer of drink.

Now, after a decade, there's this symmetry
at least: thrown back on his first wife's settee
by his marvellous, daft sod's régime ("hard
work, hard drinking and hardly sleeping") – up
for work at five, pub twelve till two, work till six, pub
again at eight, eat, then the *petit caporal*
catnap – old as a conker tree, still charming
birds from the trees like the years gone AWOL.

FROM A SHORT HISTORY OF HAIR

I NOSFERATU

Blanked by her looking-glass, he hits the bottle.
Did he start dropping out
when she dropped him? Touches

her wig-block; sighs, a reverse *Aristotle
Contemplating a Bust of Homer.*

II SESQUICENTENNIAL

Scalping
was introduced almost at once
to the Americas

by bounty hunters. More gifts followed;
pox, Christianity, guns, the hair of the dog.

III PSYCHOLOGY

A beard sports your genitals on your face –
in this, as ever, glum Freud
spoke from experience. So chant a kaddish

for your mop, chin out. A laddish
future of excess testosterone quips awaits.

IV SLAPHEADS

There, with Scargill's stately pleasure dome
go Robert Robinson and Shakespeare –
goes my father, recalling

Borges on the Falklands War:
Two bald men fighting over a comb.

v POLL TAX

Masolus, King of Caria,
had the heads of his subjects shent
forcibly, and wigs made. The prices

at which they then had to buy these back
were, to be quite frank, exorbitant.

vi SACRED AND PROFANE

Pre-Raphaelite Christ's coppery bush;
Medieval Christ's ship's captain's full set;
historical Christ's clean-shaven, fringed decorum,

like Brando's Antony. The Forum,
seething, suddenly hushed.

vii AMBITION

King Harald Fine-Hair, son of Helfdan the Black,
son of Gudrod the Hunter-King,
son of Halfdan the Open-Handed-but-Inhospitable,

until he had subdued the whole of Norway
refused to comb or cut a single lock.

viii PHILOSOPHY

Schopenhauer thought beards
politically unacceptable to the State.
His reason? That behind them,

all too easily, can lurk
the subversive and the degenerate.

ix HEARTFELT

Drops not *out* so much as *through* –
through eyebrows, ears, nape, who knows where?
When they cut open Aristomenes

of Messena, slayer of 300 Spartans,
they found a heart of pure hair.

X UNDERGROUND

Of the 180 sacks'-worth a night
collected by the Fluffers
most is human hair. Occasionally,

from beneath the third rail, they can scrape
a single piece the size of a blanket.

XI NATURAL REMEDY

Try essence of kelp with nettle-lather
over grated parsnip, sage and peach leaves.
Smear on the pate, leave for three days

then repeat. If this fails,
have words with your father.

XII ETYMOLOGY

In 336 B.C.
after the sack of Rome by the Gauls,
the Romans had erected

a temple to a pilgarlic Venus
('Caesar' means 'hairy').

XIII CROWNING GLORY

Virile oaks, bays, thorns turn over an old leaf…
The age of Chatterton, Keats – Christ!
Imagining them bald is beyond me, *a man*

of sorrows (from Handel's century of shaved heads),
and acquainted with grief.

THE YEAR OF LIVING DANGEROUSLY

'Untung was unlucky in being captured in a bus named
"Lucky" from Tegal to Semarang…'
                    – Tarzie Vittachi, *The Fall of Sukharno*

'In Mecca, Allah is closer than your jugular vein'
                    – Arab Proverb

"Nobody knew Bung Karno – not your flat tyre army,
not NASAKOM, not *kiaji*. Nobody.
If we ever guessed his next move we were lucky.
Puppet-master of all the shadows
cast on heaven's screen, when the blade
came down on us he must have been unwell.

You claim ghosts cried revenge from the Crocodile Well,
but they talked through their bollocks; just army
people turning like lazy fan-blades,
or gamelans strung to the gods. Nobody
was meant to hear. *Smoke always shadows
fire, dust blooms a mirror*. You stopped 'Lucky'

and my luck ran out, not history. A Lucky?
Thanks. A match? I see perfectly well
what you want – names, addresses, shadows
to gorge the Dwarf who heads your *wayang* army,
and wants the perfect crime – no body.
Don't be fooled; we rise in each new grass-blade.

'Don't waste bullets,' the imams say, 'draw a blade
down the pinched artery. Feel luck,
slice with the grain of the blood. Then nobody
can botch the job – the wound wells
up and runs, unhealing, and the army
knows one more goat has been skinned with shadows.'

But this mujahid won't save them. The Shadows,
lipstick, Coke – they twist a *golok*-blade
for every 'Khalimat!' choked by the army.
The necolim never dreamt they would be so lucky.
It's water from the womb to them. It's – well,
if you Farouk the Bung you'll be nobodies.

So: give me a fair trial now and kill me, nobody
can stop you. Run amok, murder shadows
heroes-in-socks... You will die as well.
Stormkings light your massacres, but blades
are *belum*, 'Yes' whets 'No'. Be unlucky
just once and you're finished. Army or no army."

No infidel body could be buried; the army
let rivers clog, and wells. They had been lucky.
Shadow-archipelagoes scabbarded their blade.

SOHO

'I never thought of a Girl as a possible event...
however, I bore the sex with great fortitude.' – Coleridge

The map had misled him all round the Wrekin.
When he asked his road at the cottage door
a hag appeared whose ugliness was soul-gelding
enough to chill a cantharidized satyr

to eternal chastity. But angel choirs
of light could hardly have been more civil
to a Pantisocratic Unitarian devil;
next day he dripped manna for seventy score –

sky-blue topcoated, lank hair unpowdered –
where King and Country mobs smoked Priestley out.
Even his fleas were citizen-philosophers,
emigrant 'live nits' from a Welsh democrat.

He fanned the congregation to slippery heat,
yet lost a tallow chandler's subscription –
a morning's recital of 'Religious Musings'
quenched by a face as long as Livery Street

and "Who watches *The Watchman* then? Spy Nosy?"
A Lunatic cicerone'd him to Hockley Brook
and the Soho Undertakings. They were stickier
than the snug in the Salutation and Cat.

Beam engines nodded, dully. Cylinders spat.
His thought flowed like water; but this was steam,
it hissed insinuation: "I offer what
the whole world desires, Sir – power!" And if

64

the condenser was not Faith, the governor Hope,
or Charity parallel motion…? Steam embossed
and blistered the seal of a note from Stowey
he had pocketed unread from the morning post

that began, *Dearest Samuel* (like her,
sun and planet gears seemed to revolve his name,
cogs tooth-kissing), *the midwife just came
in time to take away the after-birth.*

FROM THE REALMS OF GOLD

Your letters that May open, *Dear Idiot Child;*
sheets black-and-blue as share values, thin
as academic airs, they gasp at the height
of gold a thousand an ounce on the Hang Seng –
Tito didn't have a left leg left to stand on,
Brezhnev had just sneezed – Aaaf-*GHANistan!*
Everyone coined it; your bagged and Grimly
Feendish eyes glazed like a T'ang vase. Only
George, in Spain, lost out; catching the *Sun*
two days too late, he rang his trainees: 'Boss?
We sold the lot!… What do you mean, *latest* price?'

The Trade tintinnabulated – antique pots
and cruets tomahawked for cash, salvers
flattened, smelted to a bullion slaver
as Finals loomed through Hobsbawm's chapter
on 'Art and Revolution', *Silver Poets
of the Seventeenth Century* and Keats;
that summer, everything was out on a limb –
once, through sferics, a news bulletin
reported B52s up for The Rapture
before their récall: I gave up there and then
giving up on the Taste of the Big Country.

In near-war you sent the sinews of war
wrapped in advice, old Shakespeare notes –
the kind with foil – for books, beer and fish:
*Phosphorous feeds the synapses. Grow some!
Work, but beware Reverse Midas Syndrome.
Drink, but beware the dreaded Korsakov's
Psychosis – I once read the whole of James,
a chapter a night after the pub, and forget
now whether it was Henry, Joyce or Jesse.
A great author each winter, too (ah, son –
that terrible Winter of Dostoyevsky!)*

Up like a rocket. Down, slowly, like the stick,
or toasts in your Black Velcro (half Guinness,
half cider). And not five, not ten or fifteen years
would have kick-started those K-Tel Thirties,
all South Sea Bubble and the Rotters XI,
fields of cloth-of-gold that turned pyrites
where we bit-parted, Eisenstein's extras...
You sign off *Yours Auriferously* and croak
like some stormcrow, unable to resist
a grinning *P.S I would have given
my right arm to have been ambidextrous.*

QUEENSTOWN
for Alex Davis

St Colman's spire, impaling old hurts
unspiked the Titanic's last liquid parish –
its bare, slabbed inconveniences withhold
relief from those who kneel to Stella Maris –
yet the grey scree of a town dropped from its skirts
is a soft ambush; a man who drops his guard
might let sea-lavender unclench his head,
or consider reading Hart Crane in the bath.
So let those poets whose other names are death
run harmlessly to seed, tobacco and beer
in these temperate tropics – though, on the whole,
you'd rather be in Philadelphia,

although the road here twists to shake the hue
and cry of ten years of *Boutez en avant*,
the black Anubises, wolfhounds that squat
on demesne gates. Let their claws blunt with rot;
Fota collapses down its laurelled drives
where fortune squandered 'The Magnificent'
under a bend sinister (famine sold
off his hacks and oxymoronic steam yacht –
although Cork-Cobh trains would be compelled
to halt for Smith-Barrys). The wildlife park
and arboretum still gloss each tenant,
but prove you can't step in the same river once.

And what was it you saw, once, from the train,
gibboning through trees? You left from Cobh, true,
but for five seconds those woods were Malibu-
surreal, mistaken, like the Cockney who believed
he was being addressed as 'Sir', not 'so',
for weeks. We're the exotics on display,
not MacSwiney's haggard mask, McCurtain's pipes,
the museum's wall map of Crossbarry
that winks green fairy lights for the Cork Brigade
(they drilled past wet-gulched Tans laid out like game).
Perhaps Iro-Anglish, our identities
Irished like Cove to its nonce-Irish name,

are dissolving gently as the town shuffles
down through fuming roofs in the Deck of Cards.
Its house-fronts sport a *flaneur*'s orchid pinks,
blues and yellows; they drop to the sea, tides
that mooch among teabags and mackerel guts
opposite Aeneas Lane's. Past the palms,
Crimea cannon, joyrider's Alcatraz,
lie butter mountains anchored in the offing,
a blast furnace deliquescing in mist,
reflections of ideal disorder; like
some new species of consecrated bread
they are cast on the waters of Passage West.

I SAW A CITY

'Baby' Austins, bakelite, machine tool machines –
production of the production of the means

of production. Down aisles in finned temples,
Deutsch's Odeons, usherettes usher in

the spectatorship of the proletariat. At
Elmdon Airport (modelled on Tempelhof)

it rises from depression – climbs, banks
at the Municipal, hauls the country to its feet –

yet is thanked by no-one. The Prince
of Darkness has grasped electricity.

Primitive plastics begin to form. The car
as a form of worship glows and ripens

in groves of Hore-Belisha. The arcs
of estates sweep out now, twelve to an acre –

the size of Shrewsbury but with just two pubs –
their radials kissing at a raw terminus.

Summer Lane that wore Gold Standard shoes.
will pawn its suits, rings and insults

to uproot. Soon, their statesman's son's war
will gleam like the word 'fuselage' and reports

sell out: *When We Build Again*; Beveridge;
ex-Lord Mayor Tiptaft's *I Saw a City*.

KING CRIMSON

i.m Peter Hellings

So you retired to sonnets and Gauloises –
to twist blue smoke into four-square verse
(but undone by sonnets not tobacco) –
who came through the blitz-fires whole; a hero
unscathed for meat-packing, via Durban,
to fight a Phony War by gramophone
in Jerusalem's Arab Y.M.C.A.
With your best friend, the Red Jewish Atheist,
you'd spin the Fifth's black vertiginous chords
which launch your posthumous form of words –
for hadn't you, encouraged to digress,
damned Brahms as *ersatz* Beethoven in class?
You ate Birmingham like the cabbage stalk,
DJ turned D.J.. Then, near-Dylan no more,
in a Grammar-Tech pure as driven C.P. Snow
out of the years of white heat stop-go,
Trotsky-goatee'd, irascibly modest,
you opened a door on your favourites:
Andrew Young; *Twenty-Five Poems*; Yeats;
the blood-red effrontery of a *Wake*
(yours, in that year's 'A'-level prospectus,
was to scorn a merger with the girls' school
and fling down Kung's words; 'a man of fifty who
knows nothing/Is worthy of no respect').
You banned elephant collars. You disclosed
your versions of Villon. You exploded
at Jez Ready's novel interpretation
of 'trailing clouds of glory do we come'
and, once, you stormed the Sixth Form Common Room,
mental, to tear the stylus from *King Crimson*.
Who felt you *englyn*, English destiny,
too intricate for a flattered-surly
son with no fathers left to kill? 4F
will murder *Henry IV*. Hal to your Falstaff,
I heard the wolf-howl, the barked mock-reproach;
"Don't *gabble* it, boy! *Welish* it..." "Sir...?"
"'*Look*, how he *l*ards the *l*ean earth as he goes.'"

NOTES

p.14 THE EMPIRE OF ENGLISH Sir Walter Raleigh here isn't the poet, but the eccentric and self-loathing holder of the first Oxford Chair of English in the 1910s and 1920s.

p.17 A BESTIARY – 'WREN'; *droleen* is the Irish for 'wren'. 'SEAL-POINT SIAMESE'; 'Si' and 'Am' are the two Siamese cats in Disney's *The Lady and the Tramp*.

P.21 BOSOLA IN LOVE Consists of cuts made from the text of Webster's *The Duchess of Malfi* for a production by the dedicatee.

p.29 TINTERN ABBEY Another Tintern Abbey exists in Co. Wexford.

p.34 ONE OF THE PTOLEMYS Based on Thackeray's account of a visit to Cork in his *Irish Sketchbook*, published two years before the Famine and in the early stages of his wife's madness.

p.36 HARRIET SMITHSON'S JULIET Harriet Smithson was the actress with whom Berlioz fell violently in love; I and III are in his voice, II in hers.

p.42 THE CHIEF ENGINEER The subject is the architect of the Soviet space programme, who was proposed for a Nobel Prize after the Sputnik success, but whose existence was denied by Khruschev on the grounds of state secrecy.

p.48 THE KALIF OF CONAMARA *Sean-nós* is a form of Irish traditional singing likened to that of Berber Arabs; a *púcán* is a small sailing boat; *shamrukh* is Arabic for a triform leaf; *immrama* are travel tales; *Issa* and *Iosa* are Arabic and Irish respectively for Jesus.

p.50 A BIRMINGHAM YANK Term for a returned emigrant who claims to have made his money in America but has only been as far as England. Henry Ford was born in the hamlet of Ballinascarthy, Co. Cork, moving to the USA at the age of five.

p.53 EIGHTEEN EIGHTEEN *Rampions* – wild garlic; *Yola* – a Fingallian dialect of the Irish east coast, derived from West Country English (Keats's ancestors were from Somerset); *butcher's apron* – Irish republican term for the Union flag; *Sea's Swallow* – a maelstrom off the North Antrim coast. For Keats's account of his visit to Belfast, see his letter of 3-9th July 1818.

p.69 QUEENSTOWN *'Boutez en avant'* – roughly translated as 'Kick your way to the top' – is the motto of the Smith-Barry family, who stipulated that every train using the line which was built across their land had to stop at their station, just in case any member of the family wanted to jump aboard. Ireland's contribution to the EU butter mountain is in the freezer ship anchored off Cobh, formerly Queenstown.